NOW THEN,
CHARLIE ROBINSON

ff

NOW THEN, CHARLIE ROBINSON

Sylvia Woods

illustrated by
Susan Hellard

faber and faber
LONDON · BOSTON

First published in 1987
by Faber and Faber Limited
3 Queen Square London WC1N 3AU

Photoset by Parker Typesetting Service Leicester
Printed in Great Britain by
Redwood Burn Ltd Trowbridge Wiltshire
All rights reserved

Chapter I, 'Charlie Plans a Maths Lesson', first appeared in
Fighting in Break and Other Stories, edited by Barbara Ireson,
published by Faber and Faber Limited.

British Library Cataloguing in Publication Data

Woods, Sylvia
Now then, Charlie Robinson.
I. Title
823'.914[J]   PZ7
ISBN 0-571-14932-4

Contents

Charlie Plans a Maths Lesson

'I'm going to be a landlady,' said Mrs Robinson.

'What's a landlady?' asked Charlie, who was scraping up the last of his cornflakes.

'I know,' said Lucinda. 'You let rooms to people.'

'But we haven't any spare rooms,' said Charlie.

'There's Gran's room,' said his mother. 'I'm letting it for three weeks to a student teacher who is coming to your school for teaching practice. She was going to stay at the farm, but Mrs Ford is booked up with summer visitors, so I said we'd have her.'

'Is a student teacher someone who's learning to teach?' asked Lucinda.

'Yes,' said Mrs Robinson. 'Now, have you finished, you two? It's time to get the car out.'

As soon as they arrived at school, Lucinda ran off to tell her friends in the Top Juniors, where Sir taught, all about the student who was going to stay with them. Charlie joined the Lower Juniors, who were racketing about in the lobby, and swapped his Cadbury's Flake with Tim Crossman's Mars Bar before Miss Clarke called them into the classroom. She sat at her desk collecting dinner money, as she did every Monday morning. When she had taken Charlie's envelope, she told him to go and tidy the Nature Table.

'It's your turn today with Robert,' she reminded him.

Charlie and Robert were friends. They liked the same things and hated the same things. One of the things they hated was doing the Nature Table.

'Nature's silly,' said Robert.

'All flowers and growing beans and mustard and cress and all that muck,' said Charlie.

There were eight pots of very dead flowers, and the blotting paper had dried up round the runner beans. The bell for Assembly rang before they finished, so they left the flowers to droop still lower in their jars and filed out with the rest of the Lower Juniors into Sir's classroom.

As Charlie passed the piano, he managed to trip Lucinda, who was putting the hymnbook on its stand. She fell on to the keys and made a massive

crash of discords that sounded like Stravinsky.

'Carefully, carefully,' said Sir, who hadn't seen exactly what happened. Lucinda glared at Charlie but he was looking the other way.

After prayers and a hymn, Sir told them about the student, and Charlie pricked up his ears.

'. . . She will be coming on Thursday to visit the school and get to know us. Then she will return to College, but later on she will be back for three weeks to do some teaching. I am sure you will do your best to make her welcome and that I can count on all of you not to let yourselves down by bad behaviour.' He paused to look hard at a few of the Lower Juniors, and Lucinda knew which ones he was looking at.

'Right,' he said. 'Lower Juniors, return to your class.'

Back in the Lower Juniors classroom the place buzzed with excitement, because Miss Clarke said that the student was going to teach them. There was more excitement when Charlie announced that the student would be staying in his house.

'Cor, I wouldn't like a teacher staying with me . . . oh sorry, Miss Clarke,' said Annie Thomas, who always put her foot in it. 'Why can't she go on living at the College?' she asked quickly.

'Because it's thirty miles away and too far for the coaches to get them all out to country schools like ours in time to be here at nine o'clock,' explained Miss Clarke.

Thursday came, and their student arrived in a minibus. Her name was Miss Thompson, and she and the Lower Juniors spent the morning getting to know each other. Annie Thomas thought she was 'ever so nice' and Carol Davies liked the way she did her hair. Charlie hated her. It was all because she asked to look at his English book. His English book was very private. He knew he couldn't spell and so did Miss Clarke, but he didn't see why he should let Miss Thompson into the secret.

'Where's your English book, Charlie?' she asked.

'Dunno,' said Charlie.

'Well, it can't be far, can it?' She began poking around in Charlie's drawer.

Charlie stopped her. 'I'll look,' he said. He messed about in his drawer, turning books over and hoping she would go away. By mistake, the English book came up on top, and before he could send it to the bottom again, Miss Thompson pounced.

'Here it is,' she said and sat on his table turning the pages. At last she handed the book back. 'Thank you, Charlie,' she said. She opened her notebook and wrote a few things in it. All that Charlie could see was his name at the top of the page, then lots of writing he couldn't manage to read. She was probably writing about how dumb he was.

'What are your hobbies?' she asked after she had been writing for a bit.

'I dunno,' said Charlie.

If Miss Thompson had asked him what things he most liked doing, he would have known what she meant. He could have told her about fishing from the bridge with Robert and Tim, about collecting spiders and stones and shells and sticking pictures of his favourite popstars in a scrapbook. But she didn't ask him that.

'Do you like reading?' she asked.

'No,' said Charlie.

'Do you like anything?' asked Miss Thompson.

'Spiders,' said Charlie, and he was going to tell her about his collection of super whoppers in the tool shed at the bottom of the garden when she turned away.

'She's daft,' said Robert, who had been listening in.

'I hate her,' said Charlie. 'I wish she wasn't coming to live with us.'

When Miss Thompson came to stay, later in the term, Mrs Robinson arranged for all the family to have a meal together in the evening. Charlie didn't say a word all through supper although his mother tried to include him in the conversation.

Miss Thompson had lots to say to his mother and father. She made them laugh when she told them funny things that happened at College, and she talked about the College tutors as well. These were the teachers whose job was to show the students how to teach. There was one she was really afraid of. Her name was Miss Follyfoot. If she thought her students weren't good enough, they had to leave College and find a different job.

On the way to school in the car next morning, Lucinda was very talkative. She described how the school was run by Mr McKay, 'Sir' to everyone except the teachers, and what the classes were like. The Top Juniors were the best, the Infants weren't bad for babies, and the Lower Juniors, in spite of having a good teacher, were the end, and she was sorry for Miss Thompson. Charlie glared, but said nothing.

Miss Thompson didn't take the whole class for lessons during the first week, only the top group, but she used to read a story to the class at the end of each day. She read about Robin Hood and sometimes let them act bits of it, and she chose Charlie to be Robin. Charlie grudgingly admitted to himself that she wasn't bad, and by the end of the week, he wished he was in the top group. They were doing all sorts of unusual things with her. They visited the church and went to the top of the tower with Mr Patterson the Vicar. Then they went round the graveyard to look at the tombstones, to find out which were the oldest.

Twice they sat on the pavement outside the school and did traffic counts, and one afternoon Miss Thompson took them across to the village shop to buy flour, sugar, margarine, raisins and candied peel to make buns.

Charlie began to like Miss Thompson. She told him one day at breakfast that Miss Follyfoot had discovered some wrong spellings in her notebook.

'Can't you spell either?' asked Charlie.

Miss Thompson grinned. 'Not always,' she said.

Charlie could see that she was terrified of Miss Follyfoot, and each time her tutor came everything went wrong, even with Miss Clarke and all the top group willing it to go right.

It made Miss Thompson very miserable. 'She never comes to the good lessons,' she told Charlie's mother.

'You must stop being afraid of her,' said Mrs Robinson. 'Forget about her. Pretend she isn't there.'

'I can't,' said Miss Thompson. 'As soon as I see her I go all tight inside. I know everything will go wrong and it does.'

During her second week in school, Miss Thompson taught the whole class and they loved it. But they could be sure that if a science experiment failed to work or if paint water was spilt or an important book went missing, it would happen when Miss Follyfoot was there.

At the end of the week, Miss Follyfoot said she was coming in on the following Wednesday morning and she was bringing the Principal of the College with her.

'That must be because I'm so awful,' Miss Thompson told the Robinsons at tea-time. 'The Principal hardly ever goes out to see students unless there's something wrong with them.'

'What are you going to teach when they come?' asked Mrs Robinson.

'She says I've got to do a Maths lesson,' said Miss Thompson. 'I don't know what I shall do. Most of the class are doing individual work and need lots of help.'

'Do something they can all manage,' Charlie heard Miss Clarke say to Miss Thompson the next day. 'Like measuring. The top group understand about radius and diameters, so let them measure bicycle wheels on Wednesday and they can try to find out about circumferences. The middle group can have the big tape measures for doing perimeters and areas. Now the lower group are a bit of a problem . . .' Then Miss Clarke noticed Charlie. 'You get on with your work card, Charlie,' she said. 'Miss Thompson will be with you in a moment.'

On Friday evening Miss Thompson began making a set of sum cards which the lower group could use the following Wednesday. Charlie watched her and thought they were very dull. Each card had two coloured lines of different lengths drawn on it. The lines were labelled A and B. Each card had a sentence which said: 'Measure line A and line B. Which line is longer and by how much?'

'Even the dumbies in the lower group will be bored out of their minds doing those,' said Charlie when he and Robert met in the Robinsons' tool shed later that evening.

'Well, we can't do anything about it. She'll have to fail, that's all,' said Robert.

'She can't fail. It wouldn't be fair,' said Charlie. 'She can teach all right when Miss Follyfoot isn't there.'

'Couldn't we capture her and tie her up and put her in the boiler house?' suggested Robert.

'Then she'd be sure to fail if she was tied up and couldn't teach,' objected Charlie.

'Idiot,' said Robert. 'I mean tie up Miss Follyfoot.'

'She's far too big,' said Charlie. 'Haven't you seen the size of her feet and those long dangling arms? She'd clobber us before we got the rope out and anyway she's bringing some Sir with her who runs the College.'

'All right,' said Robert. 'So what do we do?'

Charlie thought. 'Measuring wheels and the playground's all right. It's the sum cards which are going to fail her. We've got to do something about those sum cards.'

'What?' asked Robert.

'I dunno,' said Charlie, 'but they ought to be jazzed up a bit.'

The tool shed was gloomy and Charlie went outside. He leant against the side of the shed and put his hands in his pockets and scuffed the ground with one foot. Robert followed him out and they both crouched down to watch a couple of worms wriggling in the dust near Charlie's feet.

'Got it!' yelled Charlie, springing up and nearly trampling on the worms in his excitement.

'Got what?' asked Robert.

'The sum cards,' said Charlie. 'Instead of measuring lines they can measure worms.'

11

'It's much more difficult measuring worms,' said Robert. 'They don't keep still, especially if you try to line them up with a ruler.'

'That's all right,' said Charlie. 'Maths is supposed to be a difficult subject.'

'Where do we get the worms?' asked Robert.

'Dig,' said Charlie. 'There must be a million in this garden.'

'We'll need to keep them somewhere till Wednesday,' said Robert.

'In matchboxes,' said Charlie. 'I've got heaps upstairs.'

Robert started digging for worms while Charlie ran indoors for his matchboxes.

'I've got thirty-seven,' he announced, coming back with a bulging plastic bag. 'Let's get thirty-seven, all sizes.'

It took some time, but at last thirty-seven worms lay in thirty-seven matchboxes. Then it was bedtime, so they left the boxes in the shed under the work bench, hidden beneath plastic sacks.

On Saturday Charlie brought out his felt-tipped pens so that they could write numbers on the boxes. Later in the day they begged a couple of pieces of coloured card from Miss Thompson and took them to Charlie's bedroom, where they cut them into thirty-seven cards. It was hard work, and the writing took them all the rest of the day, with pauses for meals. Charlie looked through the cards when they had finished.

'They'll have to do,' he said.

'Your writing's all lopsided,' said Robert.

'Yours is like a spider's with a hang-over,' said Charlie. 'Let's have a look at the worms.'

The worm in the first box they opened looked dead even when Charlie poked it.

'What's wrong with it?' asked Robert.

They opened a few more boxes and all the worms in them looked as dead as the first.

'They were all right when we put them in,' said Charlie. 'I remember number twenty-eight especially. He was a fighter. Look at him now.' He flicked worm twenty-eight and it didn't trouble to squirm. It lay where his finger had put it.

'They'll be dead by Wednesday,' said Robert. 'Fancy making all those cards for nothing.'

'I know what's wrong,' said Charlie. 'They're drying up. Do you remember in the Infants? We put them in a wormery because Mrs Bray said that worms need to keep damp.'

'We can't wet the matchboxes, they'll rot,' said Robert.

'They'll have to go in my old aquarium,' said Charlie. 'With lots of damp earth. I'll get up early on Wednesday morning and put them back in their boxes. I always hear Miss Thompson's alarm.'

They found the aquarium and put the worms in it and, thanks to Miss Thompson's alarm, Charlie managed to get the worms re-boxed before breakfast on Wednesday. They had all survived after their spell in the wormery except number twenty-eight, which Charlie decided was clinically dead and threw out of the window.

In school, everyone could see that Miss Thompson was nervous. Miss Clarke reminded them that Miss Follyfoot was coming with another visitor from the College and asked them to be on their best behaviour. It was a very hot day, so the lower group took their tables and chairs to a shady part of the playground so that Miss Thompson could keep an eye on them while she was with the other two groups doing their practical work.

They had arranged themselves outside when a car drew up. Miss Follyfoot got out with a grey-haired, jolly-looking man and they went in together to see Sir. Miss Thompson gave out her sum cards to the lower group and explained what

they had to do. She sent the middle group to start measuring the playground and then settled down with the top group, who were measuring bicycle wheels.

'Come on,' said Charlie.

He and Robert went over to the lower group, who were busily measuring lines A and B at their tables under the big chestnut tree. Out of the corner of his eye Charlie saw Miss Follyfoot and the Principal come to the school door. Robert was already collecting in Miss Thompson's cards and giving out the ones he and Charlie had made.

'You can work in two's if you like,' said Charlie

as he handed round the matchboxes. 'And there are more cards and boxes,' he added, putting the spares on the ground beside Annie's table.

'Charlie and Robert, aren't you supposed to be measuring the door?' said Miss Thompson.

They hurried towards it and stepped politely aside as Miss Follyfoot came down the steps.

'It's all right,' she said. 'Go on with what you're doing. I've only come to watch. What are you . . .?' She stopped because a scream from Annie Thomas came across the playground, followed by more screams from Carol Davies. There was sudden uproar from the whole lower group. Johnnie Norbut started to chase Susan Carter round the playground with two worms dangling from his fingers. Annie Thomas stood on her chair and Carol Davies demanded Miss Clarke at the top of her voice. A table was knocked over and Jenny Biggs was having hysterics, screaming that Christopher Dodds had dropped a worm down her dress.

Sir, Miss Clarke and Mrs Bray collided in the doorway as they came to see what had happened.

'Hey!' yelled Charlie. 'Stop treading on those boxes. You'll kill the worms.' He ran over to where Johnnie Norbut was jumping up and down in front of Susan Carter, who was crouching behind the overturned desk screaming blue murder.

'Get your foot off those boxes,' shouted Charlie.

'You shut your mouth!' yelled Johnnie, giving Charlie a thump in the eye. Charlie landed a punch on Johnnie's nose and it began to bleed. Johnnie kicked Charlie and the two of them rolled over and over on the ground until they were lifted off each other by the Principal and Sir.

Charlie shook himself as well as he could while he was still being gripped in the Principal's firm hand. Then the school and the playground and the chestnut tree stopped whizzing round and everything came back into focus. Miss Thompson looked as if she was going to cry. Charlie didn't want to cry. He was mad. Mad with Johnnie Norbut for running about chasing people with worms instead of measuring them. Mad with the whole of the lower group for messing up the lesson and making Miss Thompson fail.

When order had been restored, it was Miss Follyfoot who asked Sir to let Charlie explain and the Principal seemed as interested as she was to hear his story. From the look in Sir's eye, Charlie knew that he wanted to slipper both him and Johnnie

Norbut so hard that neither of them would be able to sit down comfortably for a week. But Sir had to be polite to visitors, so he sat and listened while Charlie told them how Miss Thompson had thought that Miss Follyfoot was going to fail her, and how he and Robert had worked so hard all week-end to make the lesson a success.

When he had finished, Sir punched his hands together. 'Well I'm da . . . er . . . well I'm blessed,' he said, and forgot all about slippering people.

The Principal was laughing and Miss Follyfoot had a grin on her face which made her look quite human. The Principal turned to Miss Thompson. 'If you can inspire such devotion in your pupils, you can't be that bad,' he said. 'Don't worry, no one's going to fail you.'

Miss Follyfoot turned to Charlie and Robert. 'It was very kindly meant,' she said. 'But I think you had better let teachers plan their own lessons in future.' Her face changed. 'You weren't thinking of being teachers yourselves when you grow up?'

'No, Miss Follyfoot,' said Charlie and Robert in horror.

'Thank goodness for that,' said Miss Follyfoot.

Charlie and the Jumble Sale

'We're having a jumble sale for the Save the Children Fund,' said Lucinda as she and Charlie got into the car after school.

'I'll look out some stuff tonight,' promised Mrs Robinson.

They collected quite a pile of things that evening. Lucinda had given up dolls, so she brought an armful from her bedroom and dumped them on the sitting room carpet.

'What about you, Charlie?' asked Mr Robinson, looking up from the crossword he was trying to do. 'Haven't you got something in that muck heap of yours upstairs?'

'It's all mostly broken,' said Charlie. 'Honestly, Dad, there's hardly anything without bits missing.'

'What about your Action Man?' suggested his father. 'You haven't played with that for months. Is that in pieces too?'

'I might want to play with him one day,' said Charlie.

'Nonsense,' said Mr Robinson. 'If your sister can send all those dolls, you can spare one measly Action Man.'

So when the things were taken to school next day, Charlie's Action Man went too. He planned to buy it back at the sale. They couldn't stop him, and he would have given something to the Save the Children Fund.

Mr McKay was amazed to see how much turned up as the days went by. The pile of things in his office grew so large that he could hardly get inside to use the telephone, and there was soon no room for Mrs Butcher, the school's part-time secretary, to sit and type. Then Mrs Patterson, the Vicar's

wife, said that they could store it in the Vicarage, so Sir was able to use his telephone and Mrs Butcher thankfully got back to her typing.

On the morning of the jumble sale, Charlie was very thoughtful during breakfast. He was working out a plan. It involved being in the Top Junior class, where the sale was being held, just before the doors opened at three o'clock. If he could be at the toy stall at one minute to three, he would be first in the queue to buy back his Action Man. He knew that his mother was going down to the school at one o'clock to help get the stalls ready.

'Mum,' he said, 'can I come and help you with the Jumble Sale?'

Mrs Robinson looked doubtful. Then she said, 'You must work hard, do what I say and not mess about, and not bother anyone, and come to me if you aren't sure of anything.' She hoped that would cover all possible things which might go wrong with Charlie in the room.

That afternoon, Charlie made himself helpful and trotted to and fro with armfuls of things for the various stalls. The helpers had trouble with prices. Mrs Patterson had priced the things when she sorted them out in the Vicarage, but the mothers who were helping Miss Clarke and Mrs

Bray said the prices were far too low So new labels were made out and Charlie saw his Action Man rise from fifteen pence, which he could afford, to a pound, which he couldn't.

Just before half past two, Mrs Patterson and the Vicar came over to say that they had discovered another box of clothes in the Vicarage. 'We must have missed them yesterday,' apologized Mrs Patterson. 'Anyway,' she added brightly, 'I have priced them.' Then she noticed that the prices of all the other things had been changed.

'I'm sure I gave everything a fair price,' she said. 'I know it's for a good cause, but we don't want to be grasping.'

'If there's going to be a price war,' murmured the Vicar, 'I think I'd better be getting back,' and he escaped to the Vicarage.

There didn't seem much for Charlie to do and it was only twenty to three. He wandered into Mr McKay's office. He was surprised to see more clothes lying on the table.

'Mum,' he called.

'Not now,' said Mrs Robinson. 'We're busy.'

Charlie went back into the office. These things hadn't been priced yet. He turned them over. There was a full-length cherry-coloured coat which looked almost new; on top of the coat there were two cardigans and an anorak, and hanging over the back of Sir's chair was a leather jacket. Three thermos flasks stood by themselves on a side table. Charlie looked into the Top Juniors' classroom. The ladies were still very busy, and no one took any notice of him as he picked up some labels and a felt-tipped pen from the desk and took them into the next room. How much was a coat? He wrote £5 and pinned it on to the cherry-coloured coat. He decided the anorak should be £3 and the cardigans £1.50 each. He took a long time deciding about the leather jacket and then priced it at £4. The flasks looked a bit tatty, so he labelled them at 25p each.

He wanted to ask his mother if the prices were right before he put the things on the stalls, so he staggered to the doorway with the coats and looked into the classroom. It was empty, and so were the Infants' and the Lower Juniors' rooms. He couldn't think where everybody had gone. He could see a crowd of people out in the street waiting for the doors to open, so he put the things on the stalls without waiting for his mother. He laid the coats on top of the ones already there. Then, because he still felt worried about his

prices, he rearranged everything so that the things he had labelled were at the bottom.

Soon afterwards the helpers came back. They had been over to the Vicarage for a quick cup of tea.

'We're late, let's open up,' said Mrs Bray.

'I'll just lock Mr McKay's office,' said Miss Clarke, 'so that nobody goes in there by mistake and takes our things.'

'Mum,' said Charlie, 'I've put all the things out. I hope the prices are all right.'

'Don't talk to me about prices,' said his mother.

'I never want to see a price tag again. Now buzz off. I've got to get to my stall before the crowd moves in.'

Mrs Bray opened the door and apologized for the delay. Everyone stormed in, determined to find bargains. Dozens of pairs of hands rummaged through the things it had taken so long to put out. Some people tried to beat the prices down and Mrs Patterson put on her 'I told you so' look. Charlie saw a blonde lady pull out the cherry-coloured coat. She tried it on and bought it. Charlie recognized her as the receptionist at the dentist's in Westing. The anorak was sold next, but the lady who bought it took it back because it had a dirty handkerchief in the pocket. The handkerchief was removed and someone else bought it. Two women almost came to blows over the leather jacket and while they put it down to argue about it, a third woman came along and snapped it up. Charlie watched the cardigans being sold and then went to look for his Action Man, but it had gone. By four o'clock almost everything had been sold and most people had left. By half past four it was all over and the grown-ups collapsed into chairs.

'I think we could all do with a nice cup of tea,'

said Mrs Patterson. 'Come on over with me.'

'What about the clearing up?' asked somebody.

'Afterwards,' said Mrs Patterson firmly. 'Let's have tea.'

Miss Clarke stood up. 'I'll unlock the door of Mr McKay's office,' she said 'so that you can collect your things.'

Mrs Robinson turned to Charlie. 'You go home now, Charlie. Thank you for being so helpful. Tell Daddy I'll be home about half past five.' She grinned and produced his Action Man from her handbag. 'Don't tell anyone, but I bought him back for you.'

'*Thanks*, Mum,' said Charlie. He'd had no idea his mother knew how he felt about his Action Man.

Then uproar broke out in Sir's office.

'Where's my coat? I know I left it on that table.'

'My jacket. Where's my leather jacket?'

'My anorak's missing.'

Charlie felt that his legs had ceased to be moveable parts of his body.

'Go on, Charlie,' said Mrs Robinson. 'I don't think you're included in Mrs Patterson's tea party. Whatever's going on in there?' She walked towards Mr McKay's office and she soon found out. All the people who had left their coats and other belongings in the room had come back to find them missing.

'But I locked the door,' said Miss Clarke.

'Anyway,' said Mrs Patterson, sounding shocked, 'I hardly like to think of thieves in the village.'

'Well, where are our things?' asked Mrs Dodds. 'That leather jacket cost a fortune. Mr Dodds bought it for me a couple of weeks ago. I daren't tell him it's gone.'

'But they can't have disappeared into thin air,' said Mrs Bray, who was looking for her fawn cardigan.

'Mum,' Charlie pulled at his mother's sleeve.

'Charlie, this is nothing to do with you,' said Mrs Robinson.

'But Mum . . .'

'GO HOME!' Mrs Robinson gave Charlie a little push.

'I sold them.'

'Look, Charlie, there's a bit of trouble here and it would be much better if . . . you WHAT?'

'I sold them.' Charlie's voice was no more than a whisper. They crowded round him, all talking at the same time.

'They were in this room,' said Charlie miserably, 'and I thought they had been forgotten like the ones Mrs Patterson brought over from the Vicarage. So I wrote some price labels and pinned them on and took them to the stalls and . . .'

'How much did you sell that leather jacket for?'

'Four pounds,' said Charlie.

'Seventy-five that coat cost.' Mrs Dodds looked round angrily. 'I hope somebody's insured against this, because I shall want compensation.'

Mrs Bray took charge. 'There has been an unfortunate mistake,' she said. 'Obviously, when everything is explained, the people who bought them will return them.'

'But who bought them?' asked one of the mothers. 'Tell me that.'

The mother who had looked after the clothing stall spoke up. 'It was that person who's just come into the village who had the leather jacket,' she said. 'You know, the one with the grey hair and the Boxer dogs.'

'I'm going up there right away,' said Mrs Dodds.

'Let's track them all down first if we can,' said Mrs Bray.

'The lady who works at the dentist bought the

red coat,' said Charlie. 'I saw her. And Johnnie's mother bought the anorak.'

'Mrs Crabbe was saying what a bargain the white cardigan was,' said Mrs Patterson. 'And I bought the thermos flasks. Of course, I shall give them back.'

'That leaves my fawn cardigan,' said Mrs Bray.

'Mrs Thomas bought that,' said Charlie.

Mrs Bray and Mrs Dodds went round to reclaim the clothes and give people their money back. Charlie went home and waited for his mother to return. He was too worried to eat his tea.

At last Mrs Robinson came in. 'Charlie,' she said, 'you'll be the death of me.' She collapsed laughing into a chair. 'Lucinda, I want a strong cup of tea. Mrs Patterson's was like dishwater.'

Charlie looked at his mother. 'You aren't cross?'

'Of course not,' said Mrs Robinson. 'You're a born chump, but you mean well.' She looked at the rest of the family. 'If only you could have seen Ma Dodds' face when she heard her precious leather jacket had been sold for four pounds.'

Charlie came and sat at the table. He reached out for a slice of bread. 'Pass the peanut butter, please,' he said. 'I'm hungry now.'

Charlie Robinson, Detective

'Mum, there's a cow in the chimney.' Charlie knelt in the hearth and peered carefully up into the darkness. 'I think it's stuck, it's mooing something terrible.'

'Oh don't talk such nonsense,' said his mother, who had just plugged in the vacuum cleaner. 'Get on with those ashes and mind the rug.'

The vacuum cleaner was switched on, and the sound of mooing was lost in the swish-roar, swish-roar as his mother pushed the cleaner over the sitting room carpet. But when Mrs Robinson carried it upstairs to do the bedrooms he could hear the cow once more. He left the hearth and stood in the middle of the room. The noise was still definitely coming from the chimney. He looked out of the window at Mr Ford's milking parlour. The cows had been milked at six o'clock that morning and the herd was now in the Back Field, enjoying the October sunshine.

'Charlie, have you finished those ashes?'

'No, Mum, and there *is* a cow up there. Shall we call the Fire Brigade?'

'You just get the hearth cleaned and then come and tidy your room. How am I expected to vacuum with your stuff all over the floor?'

Charlie scowled. Why did grown-ups never take any notice of what you said? He knelt and carefully shovelled ashes into the old tin bucket. He hated doing the job, but his mother gave him twopence for it each weekday and threepence on

Sundays, which came to fifteen pence a week. He went outside and emptied the ashes into the big galvanized iron container his father had built to store them in. Mr Robinson was a keen gardener. 'It's good for the roses,' he had told Charlie.

Charlie wasn't interested in gardening. When he was grown up, he would concrete his garden all over and have a junk yard like Luther Lipman. Only Luther's junk yard was in a field. Grass and weeds sprouted from the windows of broken-down lorries and nettles grew along the caterpillar tracks of rusty diggers. Charlie thought it would be much more convenient to put your junk on concrete. Then, when you wanted to get a gear box or some other useful spare part, you wouldn't have to do all that weeding first.

He replaced the lid on the ash bin and went into the tool shed to put the bucket away. As he pushed the bucket under the work bench, its handle caught in the pedal of his bicycle which was propped against the wall. The bicycle teetered for a moment, then crashed down. A mudguard fell off and the handle bars twisted themselves back to front. Charlie looked at it in disgust. It was falling to pieces and was far too small for him. He wondered how much Luther would give him for it as junk. He was saving to buy a BMX so that he could join the local BMX club and go in for all the track races and learn to do all the latest stunts. Then he remembered his mother was waiting for him.

He ran indoors and picked a few pieces of Lego off the floor and put them on to his bed. Then he reached under the bed and pulled out his money box. He tipped its contents on to the duvet. There was still only one pound forty-eight pence.

Mrs Robinson came in with twopence in her hand. 'You can have this when you've cleared the floor,' she said.

Charlie scooped up more Lego, put his roller skates in the cupboard, and picked up about twenty felt-tipped pens and a dozen sheets of paper. Then his mother felt she was able to vacuum the carpet.

That evening it was cold. Mr Robinson looked at his wife. 'What about a fire?' he asked.

'Yes, it is a bit cheerless,' agreed Mrs Robinson. 'There's a firelighter all ready under the wood.'

Mr Robinson reached for the matches and was going to strike one when Charlie came to life.

'You can't do that, Dad,' he said.

'What are you talking about?' Mr Robinson

looked at Charlie and struck the match, and poked it into the wood where the firelighter was.

'There's a cow up there.'

'A what?' Mr Robinson and Lucinda spoke together. A few tiny flames began to flicker in the hearth. Then, with a little pop, the firelighter burst into bigger flames and the wood began to crackle.

'A cow,' said Charlie, looking at the flames in horror. 'Mum, you remember, I told you this morning.'

'I know you were going on about something to do with a cow,' said his mother.

'When I was doing the ashes. I definitely heard a cow up the chimney. Honest.'

'It was a cow from the milking parlour,' said Lucinda. 'How daft can you get? Up the chimney!' She snorted and curled up tighter on the sofa and stuck her nose back into her book.

'It wasn't from the milking parlour, it was up our chimney,' said Charlie, glaring at Lucinda. 'And now it's going to get hurt.'

'Don't take any notice,' said Lucinda. 'It's only another of his great make-ups.'

Mrs Robinson fetched her knitting and Mr Robinson got up to switch the television on.

Charlie was furious. As usual, nobody believed him. What would happen to the cow?

Suddenly a mooing noise came from the chimney. Mrs Robinson stopped knitting, Lucinda sat bolt upright and Mr Robinson took his hand away from the television set. They all looked at Charlie.

'Told you,' he said.

Then Mr Robinson laughed and switched on the television and Mrs Robinson took up her knitting. Only Charlie and Lucinda stared at the chimney, where they could still hear the cow, fainter now because of the television.

'That cow's on top of the hill,' said Mr Robinson. 'I expect it's one of Jonah's.'

Jonah was a farmer. He lived in a house up the hill from the Robinsons, but most of his fields were two miles away on the hill top.

'How can we hear it in our chimney?' asked Lucinda.

'When the wind is in a certain direction, our chimney acts as a funnel for all the sounds that come from the top of the hill,' explained Mr Robinson. He turned the sound down on the television. 'Listen, there's a motor bike going along the top road, and there's a tractor coming down the hill. I expect it's Jonah coming home from feeding his cows.'

'So the cow isn't in our chimney, then?' asked Charlie, just to make sure.

'Of course a cow couldn't fit in our chimney, silly,' said Lucinda.

'Well, you thought it was up there just now,' said Charlie. 'You did, I saw your face.'

'Shut up, you two, I want to hear Channel Four News,' said Mr Robinson.

A few days later thieves stole Jonah's cattle. When Jonah went up to feed them one morning, he found the field empty. The gate was wide open and there were tyre marks where a heavy vehicle had backed into the gateway. Police came and took photographs of the tyre tracks. They told Jonah that a gang was at work in the area. Two weeks went by and more farmers lost their cattle. The police thought that the thieves were taking them up the motorway and selling them in Wales or the Midlands. Jonah moved more cattle into his field and slept up there each night with his dog in a tiny tent hidden in a corner under a huge oak tree. But it was damp in the tent, and after a week Jonah caught a bad chill and had to stay at home in bed.

One night while Jonah was ill, Charlie woke up

and decided to raid the refrigerator. He couldn't sleep, so he tiptoed downstairs to find something to eat. There had been chicken for Sunday dinner and there was still a lot of meat left on the carcass. Charlie tore off several strips, found some cold Brussel sprouts and a roast potato, and put it all on a saucer that was lying on the draining board. The sitting room was lovely and warm, and the lights from the milking parlour shone through the windows. Charlie sat on the hearthrug, pulled his dressing gown tightly round his legs and wriggled his bare feet into the tufts of the shaggy pile. He popped a Brussel sprout, a piece of potato and some chicken into his mouth, making it a rule to have a piece of everything in his mouth all the time. He gave himself a refill whenever necessary. First it was another piece of potato, then a sprout, then . . . What was that? Noises were coming to him down the chimney. He stopped chewing so that he could hear better.

Something heavy was moving along the top road, then it stopped. It sounded like a lorry. Charlie heard its engine start up again but sounding different. Something to do with gears. Was it backing? The engine was switched off again. Then came the sounds of cattle mooing, and a man's shout cut short, and more mooing as if cattle were being disturbed against their will.

Charlie forgot he was supposed to be in bed. He jumped up, switched on the landing light and ran upstairs, shouting at the top of his voice, 'Dad! Dad! Wake up. Get the police. They're pinching Jonah's cattle again.'

Mr Robinson was sure that somebody was murdering the children in their beds, but once he realized there was no intruder in the house, he was very annoyed.

'Is this your idea of a joke?' he demanded. 'What are you doing up at this time of night?'

'I was hungry,' said Charlie. 'And I sat by the fire to have some stuff. But, Dad, please listen.' He dragged his father to the chimney. The cattle were still making a lot of noise and there were a few shouts.

'It's the cattle thieves, Dad,' said Charlie.

Lucinda and Mrs Robinson appeared and the whole family crouched in the fireplace to listen.

'I don't know,' said Mr Robinson.

'It is, Daddy,' said Lucinda exitedly. 'I know it is.'

'Of course it is,' said Charlie. 'Everything was quiet till I heard the lorry, and it stopped and

backed and then the cows started and there were men shouting.'

'How do you know it backed?'

'It made a different sound. Dad, I know it's them. Why don't you phone the police?'

'Please, Daddy,' said Lucinda.

'All right,' said Mr Robinson. 'But I shall feel a fool if it's a false alarm. Please, sir, I heard it up my chimney.'

He picked up the telephone and very soon he was talking to the police. He didn't mention the chimney, but said enough to convince them that

39

they ought to get there right away. He described exactly where Jonah's field was.

There was a police patrol car in the area and the driver and his partner were able to catch the thieves just as they were taking the lorry out of the field with Jonah's cattle inside it.

Jonah asked Mr Robinson what he thought Charlie would like by way of saying thank you. Mr Robinson said to forget it, but Jonah had other ideas. He had seen Charlie riding round the village on his old bike which was falling to pieces and was far too small for him, and he had a nephew in Bristol who had grown out of his bike and had recently been given another. He made the journey into town in his Land Rover and came back with his nephew's old bike. It was in excellent condition but he was a bit disappointed with it. He thought a really good bike ought to have large wheels with dozens of metal spokes and lots of gears. This one had no gears at all and small wheels with thick yellow spokes. But it looked as if it would fit Charlie better than his old one.

He brought it round to the Robinsons one evening and said he was sorry that it had funny wheels and no gears or drop handle bars but . . . then he noticed that Charlie wasn't listening. He was just staring at the bike.

'Is . . . is it for me?' he asked hoarsely. He seemed to have lost his voice. Jonah wished he'd never had the idea. 'Well, yes,' he said and started to apologize all over again about the bike's having no gears and drop handlebars. But Charlie let out a great whoop of joy and leaped on the bike and rode it up and down the lane.

'Is it really for me?' he asked again as he rode up and almost ran Jonah over.

'Do you like it, then?' asked Jonah.

'It's exactly what I wanted,' said Charlie. 'It's a super BMX. I can join the BMX club now and go racing.'

'Well, blow me,' said Jonah in a relieved voice. 'I did the right thing after all.'

Mr Robinson bought Charlie a crash helmet, jacket and gloves, and Charlie used the money he had saved from doing the ashes to join the BMX Club. Mrs Robinson still made him clean the grate and she continued to pay him twopence on week-days and threepence on Sundays. There was next year's subscription to think of, she said.

Charlie Works a Miracle

Bonnie, the spaniel who lived with the Jacksons in the big bungalow down the road, had a litter of puppies, and Charlie wanted one. There were five in the litter and a rumour was going round the village that the pups would be sold for seventy-five pounds each when they were old enough to leave their mother.

'Seventy-five pounds!' exclaimed Mr Robinson when Charlie brought the subject up at breakfast. 'Well, all I can say is that some people have too much money to throw around.'

'Could we have a dog if it didn't cost too much?' asked Charlie.

Mr Robinson looked across the table. 'You'd better ask your mother,' he said, 'She'll be the one who'll have to clear up its messes.'

'I shouldn't mind,' said Mrs Robinson, 'and the messes don't last long, only until it's house-trained.

Perhaps we could get one from the Dogs' Home.'

Charlie had nothing against dogs from the Dogs' Home, but he had set his heart on one of Bonnie's puppies. Then he heard that one of them had turned out to be much smaller than the others and would be sold for less than her brothers and sisters.

'I wonder how much it'll be,' said Charlie to Robert.

'Let's go and ask,' said Robert.

'Go and ask?' said Charlie in alarm. 'But I don't know the Jacksons. I've never been there in my life. They're very posh and horribly rich.'

'Well, you want the puppy, don't you?' said Tim, who was with them. 'I dare you.'

'All right,' said Charlie.

'You'd better go with him to see that he does it,' Tim said to Robert.

They went on Saturday afternoon. There was nobody about, and their shoes scrunched noisily on the gravel as they walked up the drive, skirted a big ornamental pond filled with huge golden fish, and climbed the three shallow steps that led to the front door.

'You ring,' said Robert.

Charlie rang and Mrs Jackson herself opened the front door. Charlie had half-expected a maid or a butler.

'Hullo,' she said. 'Is it Bob a Job week?'

'No,' said Charlie. 'We've come to see about the puppies.'

'Could we see them, please?' asked Robert.

'Of course,' said Mrs Jackson easily. 'Come in.'

She led them through the house, into an enormous kitchen fitted with every kind of gadget you could imagine, and then into another room where Bonnie was lying in a big wooden box with her puppies. She rose to greet her visitors, scattering puppies in all directions. She was black and white, and as far as Charlie could make out, two of her puppies were black all over and two were grey and

44

white with black ears. There was no sign of the fifth until a tiny white head popped up between the broad backs of two of its brothers. It looked at Charlie out of a pair of bright blue eyes and began to wriggle and squirm its way out. It seemed to be all white except for a pair of black ears and a black smudge over one eye.

'Oh, please can I hold it?' asked Charlie.

'Of course,' said Mrs Jackson, and she pulled the puppy out of the litter and plumped it down into Charlie's outstretched arms. The puppy put out a tiny pink tongue and licked Charlie's forehead as he bent his face down to it. It felt soft and warm and fitted into his hands like a silky ball. Then Mr Jackson came in.

'Ha. Visitors,' he said.

'We've come to see the puppies,' said Charlie, who felt he ought to say something.

'Are your hands clean, boys?' asked Mr Jackson. 'Can't be too careful, you know. These are valuable pups. Can't afford to take risks.'

'I washed my hands before I came out,' said Charlie, glad for the first time in his life that his mother had won the hand-washing battle they had every day in his house. 'Have they all got homes?'

'All but the one you're holding,' said Mr Jackson.

'How much would this puppy cost?' asked Charlie, and in his anxiety, his hands tightened on the dog, which let out a little squeal.

'Don't squeeze her, dear,' said Mrs Jackson, taking the puppy and putting it back in the box, where Bonnie started to lick it.

'Sixty pounds,' said Mr Jackson, 'and that's cheap. The others are going for seventy-five. But she's a good little bitch. Make somebody a fine pet.'

Charlie and Robert had nothing to say except to thank Mrs Jackson for letting them see the puppies as she took them to the front door.

'He must be joking,' said Robert when they were in the road once more.

'He wasn't,' said Charlie. 'Old skinflint. Filthy money bags. But I do want that puppy. I'm going to pray for a miracle.'

'They only happen in the Bible,' said Robert.

'They don't. My dad said it was a miracle when the Bank Manager let him have a loan to start his Driving School business.'

'Go on,' said Robert scornfully. 'A miracle's something like the loaves and the fishes.'

Weeks passed. The puppies grew up, and one by one went to live with people who could afford seventy-five pounds. Charlie wondered whether the Jacksons had managed to sell the smallest one. He stopped at their gate one evening when Mr Jackson was cleaning out his fishpond.

'Have you sold the tiny puppy yet?' asked Charlie.

'Not yet,' said Mr Jackson. 'She's called Smudge, by the way – black smudge over her eye, you know.'

'I could give her a home if you want to get rid of her,' said Charlie. 'If you drop the price a bit – quite a bit.'

'Come in if you want to talk business,' said Mr Jackson. 'And I can clean out the pond while we're talking.'

Charlie went in and stood with Mr Jackson beside the pool. The fish really were enormous, as big as the trout in the reservoir.

'Aren't the goldfish huge?' he said.

'They're carp,' said Mr Jackson firmly. 'And this little collection is worth something, I can tell you. Now, did you say your family wanted to buy Smudge?'

'How much would she cost?' asked Charlie.

Mr Jackson considered. 'Hm . . . last time I saw you I said sixty, didn't I? Well, I'll do you a favour, call it fifty-five.'

'Pounds?' said Charlie, to whom fifty-five pence was a fortune.

'Pounds,' said Mr Jackson.

'But she's very tiny,' said Charlie, 'and I thought perhaps as nobody seems to want her that you might sell her to me very cheaply. I'd take great care of her and look after her properly.'

'Look, laddie,' said Mr Jackson. 'Business is business and don't you forget it. I only got where I am now by remembering that.'

'My dad hasn't got fifty-five pounds,' said Charlie.

'Then I'm afraid you'll have to give up the idea.'

'I told Robert only a miracle would make you change your mind,' said Charlie, who was so disappointed he didn't care whether he sounded rude or not.

'Who's Robert?'

'The boy who came with me to see the puppies. He said miracles only happen in the Bible.'

''Fraid they do,' agreed Mr Jackson cheerfully.

'Letting me have your puppy for free would be a miracle that's not in the Bible,' said Charlie.

'Yes,' said Mr Jackson, 'and if the water in my carp pond turned bright green, I suppose you'd call that a miracle, but that sort of thing doesn't happen.'

'I know,' said Charlie. He turned miserably away and made for the gate.

'Tell you what,' said Mr Jackson. Charlie looked

round. 'If my carp pond ever turns bright green, I'll give you the pup for free. How's that, eh? You start praying for a miracle, my boy.' Charlie left him laughing at his own joke. He didn't see anything to laugh at and was miserable for days afterwards whenever he thought of Smudge.

He cheered up a bit near the end of term, when Miss Clarke hired a coach to take the Lower Juniors on an outing. They visited a Nature Trail on the Mendips. They had a picnic first, and then they scrambled down into a little valley where a stream was bubbling through brambles and fern over a stony bed. They followed it until suddenly it disappeared and the stony gully ran on without any water in it.

'Where's the water gone?' asked Annie Thomas.

Miss Clarke explained how lots of streams in the hills around them did that. 'They run through underground limestone passages,' she said, 'and sometimes they come out above the ground for a little way lower down the hill and plunge again under the rock and come out in the valley.'

'Like the Underground in London,' said Tim, who had been there. 'We got on at Paddington and we went through a tunnel and stayed underneath the ground for ages, but when we got to South

Kensington, where we were getting out, we were in the open air again.'

'That's right,' said Miss Clarke.

'Do the streams in Easting come through the ground like that?' asked Charlie.

'Most of them do,' said Miss Clarke.

'Gosh,' said Charlie. He took a matchbox out of his pocket (he always had a matchbox or two on him, they came in very useful) and put it into the stream. It bobbed gently along for a few centimetres and then got stuck against a stone. He lifted it off and sent it on its travels once more.

'Don't litter the countryside, Charlie,' said Miss Clarke. 'If you have anything to throw away, keep it for the rubbish box on the coach and we'll take it back to the school dustbin.'

Charlie didn't think it worth explaining that his matchbox was an experiment, that it was supposed to follow the stream through all its winding way underground until it came out one day in Easting. He picked it out of the water, dried it on his handkerchief and stuffed it back into his pocket.

He tried again when the others had all moved off and nobody was looking. This time he put the matchbox right where a stream disappeared into the ground. Nothing happened, the matchbox struck there, because there was no real opening, no black tunnel to go through like there was on the London Underground. How did people know that these streams came out into Easting and all the other places? It couldn't be done by floating things down them. He picked up his matchbox and ran after the others.

After the outing, Charlie was very busy practising for the school Sports Day and he had little time to think about the Jackson puppy. Then one day Mrs Robinson picked him up from school with Lucinda and drove off without waiting to talk to the other mothers.

'You're in for it, you are,' she said to Charlie. 'I don't know how you could do such a stupid thing.'

'Do what?' asked Charlie. 'I haven't done anything.'

'It's lucky your father was home early today,' said Mrs Robinson. 'I couldn't have coped with Mr Jackson on my own.'

She wouldn't say another word, and when they reached home, she hauled Charlie towards the sitting room, where he could hear someone speaking in a loud angry voice.

'Well, here he is,' he heard his father say.

Mr Robinson was standing with his back to the

fireplace, while Mr Jackson was pacing up and down the room. He turned on Charlie. 'What do you mean by it?' he demanded. 'How dare you? Because you and that friend of yours have visited my house, you needn't think you can . . .' Words failed him.

Charlie stood stiff and still. He reached out and clutched his mother's hand. Mr Robinson saw Charlie's white face. 'I'll ask him about it,' he said. 'Sit down, Charlie. Let's all sit down.'

Mr Jackson threw himself on the sofa and muttered something about calling the police. Mr Robinson looked gravely at Charlie. 'Do you know anything about Mr Jackson's pond?' he asked.

'No, Dad,' said Charlie.

'Of course he does,' raved Mr Jackson.

'Please,' said Mr Robinson. He turned to Charlie. 'Mr Jackson thinks you have been fooling around with his pond. Now come on, what do you know about it?'

'Nothing,' said Charlie. 'I haven't been near his pond. Honest, Dad.'

'Then he put his friends up to it,' snapped Mr Jackson.

'Up to what?' asked Charlie. 'What's been going on, Dad?'

'Mr Jackson says you've done something to the colour of his pond.'

'What!' Charlie leaped up with sparkling eyes and looked at Mr Jackson. 'Is it green?' he asked.

'You'll pay for it,' said Mr Jackson. 'Pay for the water to be pumped out, pay for the fish too if they've been poisoned.'

'Charlie, just what have you been doing?' asked Mr Robinson wearily.

'Nothing,' said Charlie. 'It's a miracle.'

Mr Jackson made a choking noise and it was another quarter of an hour before the Robinsons pieced together the story of the puppy and the miracle from the bewildered Charlie and the raging Mr Jackson. The pond had been quite normal at eight o'clock that morning when Mr Jackson left for work, but by three o'clock in the afternoon it had turned bright green. Mrs Jackson had telephoned her husband at his office and he had come home early. Mr Robinson persuaded Mr Jackson to go home and promised to telephone him in the morning. When Robert came up to play with Charlie after tea, Mr Robinson questioned them both, but Robert had no more idea than Charlie how the water had changed colour.

In school next day, Charlie kept expecting to see

53

a policeman walk in to arrest him. When school was over and he was still a free citizen, he went into Mr Ford's field below the garden to think things out and be away from Mr Jackson if he came round again. Robert and Tim came up and joined him beside the ditch.

'I wish old Jackson would drown in his rotten pond,' said Robert.

'Are you sure you didn't do it by just thinking about it?' asked Tim. 'Perhaps you've got special powers. Kine – something it's called. There was this film where a girl wanted to get her own back on everybody and she willed things to happen like a dance hall falling down on people at a disco and they all died horrible deaths like being electrocuted and having ceilings falling down on them.'

'Oh shut up,' said Charlie. 'I didn't do anything. I don't know how his beastly water turned green.'

'I say,' Robert's voice sounded very odd. 'Look, Charlie, you've done it again. The water in the ditch has turned green while we've seen sitting here.' They scooped the water out in their hands, and it was defintely green.

'It's nothing to do with me,' said Charlie.

'Are you sure you aren't willing it?' asked Tim.

'No I'm not,' snapped Charlie. He felt frightened. 'I'm going home and you needn't come.' He scrambled through the hedge and ran up the garden path. He was going to shut himself in his bedroom and not come out until all the water round the place had settled down to its normal colour.

He arrived indoors to find the house full of people. He stood miserably in the doorway of the sitting room and looked around. At least there weren't any policemen. Mr Jackson was there with Mrs Jackson, who was holding Smudge. His mother and father were there, and Lucinda, and three strangers, two young men in anoraks and an older man in a grey suit. Except for Lucinda, they were all drinking sherry. No one seemed to be annoyed any more, in fact they all looked very friendly.

Mrs Jackson smiled. 'Here he is,' she said, and turned to her husband, who came forward to stand in front of Charlie. He looked very embarrassed and didn't seem to know what to say. Suddenly, he took Smudge from his wife's arms and held him out to Charlie.

'She's yours,' he said. 'Can't go back on my word. Yours for free, like I said. But it was an odd sort of miracle. Sorry to have doubted you, old chap. Wasn't anything to do with you, it was these Johnnies here.' He indicated the three strangers. 'Anyway, look after the pup. If you want any advice, ask us.'

Charlie sat down suddenly on the nearest chair, clutching Smudge. His legs seemed to have gone wrong. The puppy reached up and licked his face.

'But what's happened?' he asked. 'The water in the ditch is green as well.'

The man in the grey suit smiled. 'That's us, I'm afraid. The Water Board.' He explained that his assistants, the two young men in anoraks, had been putting dye into the streams at the top of the hill to trace the underground water courses and find out where each one came to the surface lower down. 'We're planning to build a small reservoir in Easting and it helps us to know where all the water comes from and goes to,' he said.

One of the young men said, 'We were using red and green dyes. They're quite harmless and we have been able to reassure Mr Jackson that his fish will be all right. Their pond is fed by an underground stream which comes up in his garden, so some of the dye landed up there.'

'It might have been red,' said the other young man. 'I was using the red dye, but it was Ted's green stuff that came into Easting.'

'Of course it was,' said Charlie happily. 'It had to be green to work the miracle.'

Now Then, Charlie Robinson

It was ten o'clock on Saturday morning and Charlie had been chased out of the house by his mother, who was in one of her spring-cleaning moods. He kicked and scuffed his way to the tool shed at the bottom of the garden, but there was nothing in there to interest him. Behind the tool shed was a hedge which marked the boundary between the Robinsons' garden and one of Mr Ford's fields, and on the other side of the hedge there was a deep and murky ditch with a trickle of water in the bottom, where Charlie sometimes found grass snakes. He wondered if there were any in it at the moment, so he slipped through the hedge to have a look and squatted down in the bottom of the ditch. There was very little water, and he couldn't find anything except something the size of a caterpillar with dozens of pairs of legs, which ran away quickly when he turned over the stone it was hiding under.

As a source of wild life, the ditch was very disappointing, so Charlie did the only thing possible, he turned it into a First World War trench. He lay on his stomach with his head sticking over the top and started shooting Mr Ford's cows with a stick balanced on the edge. They scarcely noticed him and went on tearing up the grass. Charlie shouted, 'Bang . . . boom . . . ker-ump!' to let them know they were under attack. One inquisitive animal lumbered over to him and put her moist nose down to sniff his stick.

'Go away!' shouted Charlie, jumping up. 'You smell of stale milk.' He waved his stick at her, and she gave a little prance at the top of the ditch which made her great udder shake. Then she veered off down the hill towards the stream at the bottom. Some of the others followed, and Charlie climbed out of the ditch and did a war-dance that sent the whole herd cantering full pelt down the slope. Charlie could hear the ground echo to the sound of their hooves.

'Hope old Ford isn't watching,' he thought and took shelter once more in the ditch.

Whack! A clod of earth smacked down beside him, followed by a second and a third which hit him in the small of the back. He scrambled out of the ditch.

'Hey, wacherthinkyer doing?' he yelled.

'You're dead, Charlie Robinson,' said a voice and Robert stepped out of the hedge. 'Your mum said you were down the garden somewhere, and I've got Smudge. She was sleeping on Lucinda's bed and she's been turned out of the house.' Smudge and Robert joined Charlie in the ditch. 'Why were you dancing around and waving a stick about?' asked Robert.

'I was shooting Germans, wasn't I?' said Charlie.

'There's a German coming up the field now,' said Robert.

'Oh crumbs, it's Mr Ford,' said Charlie. 'Quick, get back into the garden.' They made it to the safety of the other side of the hedge as Mr Ford reached the ditch.

'Now then, Charlie Robinson,' he said, 'I was in Top Field when I saw you. You leave the cows alone, do you hear? The milking figures will be down this afternoon after the fright you've given them.'

Robert and Charlie slowly backed round the tool shed while he was speaking. He couldn't see them properly because of the hedge, and as soon as they had the shed between them and the angry farmer, they raced up the path towards the house.

'We'd better keep out of his way for a bit,' said Charlie.

'Let's go and see if Jonah wants any help,' suggested Robert.

'Good idea,' said Charlie. He stuck his head inside the back door. 'Mum,' he called. 'We're going up to Jonah's to the wood yard.'

Jonah sold logs when he had them, and Charlie and Robert used to help him load them into his trailer when he had a delivery to make. He paid

61

them twenty-five pence each per load, so it was worth it.

'If you're taking Smudge with you, keep her on a lead in case the sheep are round the house,' said Mrs Robinson, coming into the kitchen. 'And make sure you're back by a quarter to twelve. We're having an early lunch because I'm taking you to have your hair cut afterwards.'

Charlie groaned. He hated having his hair cut, because everybody at school laughed at him, even Miss Clarke. 'You look like a convict, Charlie,' she used to say, 'but never mind, you'll be all right in a few weeks when it's grown again.'

He grumbled and kicked stones about all the way up to Jonah's, and then grumbled some more because no one was at home and he had lost his chance of earning any pocket-money. There were sheep in the field beside the house, and the two miniature ponies Tipsy and Tandy, which belonged to Jonah's wife, were standing nose to tail beneath a chestnut tree, whisking the flies off each other.

'Let's ride them round the field,' said Robert. 'Which one do you want?'

'Neither,' said Charlie. 'They're unrideable.'

'You're yellow,' said Robert, and climbed over

the fence. Charlie sat on it, holding on to Smudge's lead and watched.

Robert walked up to Tandy, who stretched her nose out to see if he had something to eat, but when she found that he wanted to get up on to her back, she kicked her hind legs in the air and ran away. Then Tipsy came along with her ears back and nipped Robert's bottom, and while he was twisting round trying to see what damage she had done, Tandy came roaring into the attack and chased him to the fence. She came to an abrupt stop as Robert tumbled over into a clump of thistles.

'Told you,' said Charlie.

'Old Tipsy doesn't half bite,' said Robert as he picked himself up. 'Do you think I'll get rabies?'

'Not from horses,' said Charlie, leaving go of Smudge's lead while he pulled some of the prickles out of Robert. 'You only get it from dogs and . . . oh gosh!' He stopped talking and gasped. The sheep, which had huddled together while Robert was trying to get on to Tandy's back, were now rushing wildly to and fro as Smudge flew after them, chasing first one group then another.

'Stop her!' yelled Charlie. 'If Jonah comes now, he'll shoot her.'

They threw themselves over the fence and went after Smudge. The field was full of sheep, ponies, two boys and a dog capering madly in all directions. At last, Charlie caught Smudge by throwing himself on her as she raced past and hanging on to her trailing lead.

'Let's get out of here,' said Charlie.

They crossed the road and climbed the stile into the field opposite Jonah's house. 'We'll take Smudge into the woods and let her chase rabbits,' he said. Down in the village, the clock chimed twelve, but neither Robert nor Charlie heard it. Suddenly there was a loud roaring noise above their heads and, looking up, they saw a hot air balloon coming their way very close to the ground. It was so low that they could see the man inside the basket. They waved to him and he waved back. Smudge hated the balloon and made little dashes round the field, barking madly all the time. The pilot reached up and pulled on a couple of handles, there was another roar, and flames shot up into the balloon.

'He does that to lift it,' said Robert.

'I know,' said Charlie. 'He'll have to lift it jolly high to get over Cutt's Wood.'

They stood and watched while the balloon rose

to clear the trees, its basket almost scraping the tops of the tallest ones. Then it floated down again on the far side until all they could see was its top.

'Come on,' said Charlie, 'I bet he's going to land.'

They charged through the wood, which was just a narrow belt of trees along each side of a stream running between two fields. They saw the balloon coming in to land as soon as they were clear of the trees. Unluckily for the pilot, the ground was very uneven and sloped up steeply from the wood. At that moment a freak wind blew down the field. The pilot pulled the handles, but there was no answering roar.

'He's run out of gas,' said Charlie. 'Now what's he going to do?'

'He'll tip over,' said Robert, and he was right. The basket overturned and fell heavily on to its side. The wind pulled at the balloon, which dragged the basket bumping along the ground. Then the balloon itself started to collapse like an elongated sausage and floated on to the grass.

'Let's see if we can help,' said Charlie, as the village clock struck the quarter hour. They ran up the slope with their eyes on the basket, waiting for the pilot to climb out, but nobody appeared. Smudge arrived first and began barking and capering about on the balloon itself. A head looked out from the basket. 'I say,' it called, 'do you mind keeping your dog off the fabric?' The words ended in a groan and the head disappeared.

Charlie put Smudge on her lead and they walked round the basket. An oldish man was lying inside and didn't seem to be trying to get up.

'Have you hurt yourself?' asked Charlie.

'It's my shoulder, I think I've broken it,' said the

man. 'No, don't help me up, it hurts too much.'

'We'll get someone,' said Robert.

The man looked at him. 'Can you see a car anywhere?' he asked.

'A car?' Robert looked blankly round the fields and back at the wood.

'We're always followed by a car,' the man explained, 'to take us home when we come down.' He smiled. 'It should have been an ambulance this time.'

'I can't see a car or even hear one,' said Charlie, 'I think we'd better run home and phone for an ambulance.'

'How long will it take you?' the man asked.

'About ten minutes,' said Robert.

'Make it five,' said the man and closed his eyes.

Robert leaned forward. 'He's died on us,' he said.

'Course he hasn't,' said Charlie. 'He's still breathing. Look, his overalls are going up and down.'

'He's very green,' said Robert, peering at him. 'Shouldn't we do something?'

'Yes,' said Charlie. 'Run like heck and find a telephone.'

They took a short cut across the fields and did

the journey back to Charlie's house in six minutes. They arrived to find four indignant grown-ups waiting for them. Mr Ford had come to complain about Charlie's treatment of his cows, Jonah and his wife Wendy were there because they had seen Robert upsetting the ponies and Smudge chasing the sheep while they were on the hill with a sick heifer, and Mrs Robinson was furious because Charlie was going to miss his hairdressing appointment.

'Now then, Charlie Robinson,' they all began.

'Quick,' gasped Charlie, 'that man in the balloon. He's hurt in Two Acre Field.'

'Fainted. Might be dead,' added Robert.

'Is this some cock and bull story of yours?' asked Mrs Robinson.

'No it isn't,' said Charlie indignantly. 'Honest, Mum. He's hurt. He needs an ambulance.'

'I saw it going low,' said Jonah. 'I said to Wendy, I wonder if it's coming down.'

Mr Ford, who had disappeared as soon as Charlie spoke, came back into the room. 'I used your phone,' he said. 'There's an ambulance coming here for directions. I've got the Land Rover outside, so I'll go straight up.'

Charlie was amazed. He had never realized

how quick-thinking Mr Ford was in an emer-
gency. He always seemed to move at the same
pace as his cows, never in a hurry – except when
he was chasing Charlie off his land. He was a
different man when it really mattered. Mrs Robinson grabbed the First Aid box she always kept in
the kitchen and followed Mr Ford out to the Land
Rover. 'You two stay here and wait for the
ambulance so that you can direct them,' she told
Robert and Charlie. Then she was gone and the
boys were left with Jonah and Wendy.

'Hope the chap's going to be all right,' said
Jonah. Then he turned to Robert. 'If I ever catch
you trying to ride one of those ponies again, I'll
tan the backside off you.' He looked at Smudge.
'That's a good little bitch, Charlie, now don't you
go spoiling her by letting her run wild.'

'I've been talking to your mum about training
classes for her,' said Wendy.

Then the ambulance arrived, and Robert and
Charlie persuaded the driver that it would be very
difficult to find his way unless they came with
him, so they were allowed to climb aboard and go
with the ambulance to Two Acre Field. They
arrived at the same time as a Volvo which was
pulling a trailer. Three people got out and one of

them was the balloonist's wife, so after the ambulance men had given him an injection, and put him on a stretcher, she was able to go with him to the hospital.

The car driver said that they had been following the balloon across country but had to stop and mend a puncture. Everybody helped to fold the balloon and stow it away in its bag. It was still beautifully warm inside, and Charlie and Robert kept walking about trying to find the warmest spots, until they were told they had to help or walk home.

In all the excitement, Charlie didn't get his hair cut for another week, by which time it had grown really long. So when it was cut, he looked more like a criminal than ever, and Miss Clarke couldn't stop laughing.

While Shepherds Watched

'We're going to do a Nativity Play,' said Charlie. 'Just us, not Sir's class, and I'm going to be a shepherd.'

'Sir says it ought to be us doing the play because we're older,' said Lucinda, 'but Miss Clarke thought of it first, so it has to be you.'

'It'll be all right,' said Charlie. 'Sir's going to be knocked back when he sees it.'

The Lower Juniors worked very hard at their play. They all wanted to show Sir what they could do. Tim was St Joseph and his father made a stable with doors that opened and closed. When Tim and Jennifer Muller, who played Mary, had been settled in the stable by Robert the innkeeper, they could close the doors and the audience could forget about them until the time came for the stable to be opened again for the shepherds to visit the new-born baby.

Tim's sister Annalise, who had come up from Mrs Bray's class into the Lower Juniors that term, was an angel and Miranda Jefferson was the Black King. Her family had moved into the village a month before. They had come over from the United States, so that Miranda's mother could teach drama at the university outside Burracombe. Her father had come too, because he wrote detective stories and said it didn't matter where he wrote them so long as he was left in peace. The other member of the family was baby Dominic, who was six months old. Mrs Jefferson made herself very useful organizing a group of mothers to make clothes for the play.

'It's going to be super,' Charlie announced one tea-time. 'Just you wait.'

'It had better be,' said Lucinda. 'Sir's wishing we were doing it after all.'

'It's too late now,' said Charlie. 'There's only a week to go. What's he on about?'

'Mrs Jefferson's gone and contacted the local television people, and they're sending a cameraman on the day to take pictures. Sir doesn't know whether to be pleased or not. He doesn't know whether you lot are to be trusted not to let the school down.'

'Don't worry,' Mrs Robinson comforted her. 'It won't be broadcast live. If they don't like it, they won't put it out. They don't show everything they film.'

Charlie almost burst with indignation. 'They jolly well are going to show *us*,' he said.

The Lower Juniors were so excited at the thought of the television cameras that even Miss Clarke was a bit worried about how they would react on the day. Charlie lay awake at nights thinking about it. The play wasn't bad. They had Mrs Jefferson's super costumes and Mr Crossman's stable. He talked to Miranda about it and she told him to quit worrying, but Charlie insisted that it still needed something to make it extra special so that people would remember it for years to come. The great idea came to him on the day of the dress rehearsal. They were doing it on the stage of the village hall. When the shepherds reached the stable, Charlie had to give a sheepskin to Tim, who put it over the baby in the manger.

'Soppy-looking baby,' muttered Charlie, as he handed the skin over and watched Tim tuck it round the stiff doll with staring eyes that Annie Thomas had brought to be Baby Jesus.

'What we want is a real baby,' said Charlie to

some of the others when the rehearsal was over.

'Where'd we get one from?' asked Jennifer.

'There must be heaps of babies about,' said Charlie.

'There's a baby in the bungalow opposite the garage,' said Annalise.

'It's too big and its nose runs and it's a horrible baby,' said Tim.

'There's Dominic,' said Miranda.

Everyone looked at her. They were all thinking the same thing but nobody liked to say it. At last Tim spoke. 'He's the wrong colour,' he said.

'How do you know?' asked Miranda. 'Have you ever seen Jesus, Tim Crossman? How do you know he wasn't black?'

'He just wasn't,' said Tim. 'Jesus was a white man.'

'That's because white men wrote the Bible, I guess,' said Miranda. 'If a black man had written the Bible, Jesus would have been black.'

'No he wouldn't,' said Jennifer. 'He was a Jew, wasn't he? He came from Palestine, where Israel is today. What colour are the people who live there?' Nobody knew.

'Let's watch the news tonight,' said Jennifer. 'There's been trouble with bombs going off. If there are pictures from Israel we can see what colour the people are.'

That evening more children than usual watched the television news bulletins, and the next day, everyone agreed that people from Israel were darker than British people but not as dark as Miranda.

'So a white baby's just as wrong as a black baby,' said Miranda. 'We haven't got one the right colour, so I'll get Dominic.'

'How do we get hold of him?' asked Tim. 'You can't just walk into your house and hoik him out.'

'Yes I can,' said Miranda. 'Dad's baby-sitting while Mum comes to the play, and when Dad's writing a book, he doesn't notice whether it's Dominic or a baby elephant in the cot.'

'But suppose he does notice?' asked Tim. 'We don't want him dialling 999.'

'I'll leave a note in Domie's cot to say he's with me,' Miranda promised.

The television men moved in on the day of the play. There was a sound recordist, a cameraman and an interviewer. They talked and joked with the children while they were putting on their costumes and took pictures of them while they were getting ready for the play. At half past two, they joined the audience and the performance began. To get people in the right mood, the Top Juniors sang some carols, and while Miss Clarke accompanied them on the piano in the hall and Mrs Patterson, who had come to help backstage, was trying to keep the Lower Juniors quiet, Miranda slipped out to fetch Dominic. She returned with a sleeping bundle in her arms just as Mr Beezy the caretaker was pulling back the curtains for the Nativity Play.

'Here he is,' she whispered to Tim and Jennifer, who were waiting in the wings.

'Quiet now, dears,' said Mrs Patterson, who had no idea what was going on. 'Mr Beezy's drawing the curtain.'

The play began. There was some music from the piano, and Mary and Joseph came on looking for somewhere to stay. The innkeeper and his wife led them to Mr Crossman's stable, and Robert carefully closed the doors. While the shepherds acted their scene, they could hear whispering behind the stable doors and guessed that Dominic was being put into the crib. Behind the doors, sheltered from the lights, Dominic slept, and Tim and Jennifer waited anxiously for the moment when the stable would be opened. But when Robert drew back the doors, Dominic slept on.

'It's going to be OK,' breathed Tim, and then turned himself into St Joseph, who greeted the shepherds and thanked them for coming. He took the sheepskin from Charlie and tucked it round Dominic. The audience smiled; it was a nice idea. Then they gasped. Dominic was already hot, and a sturdy black leg came up to kick at the rug. The sheepskin slipped to one side and a white knitted bootee shot off his foot and flew across the stage. Dominic gurgled, kicked and waved his arms at Jennifer. Charlie was delighted.

Miranda peered anxiously from the wings. Would Tim have the sense to leave the sheepskin where it was? 'Leave it,' she whispered. 'He doesn't want it.' But Tim didn't hear. He decided that St Joseph wasn't the sort of person to put up with nonsense from a baby, and he tucked the rug firmly over Dominic's legs. Dominic opened his mouth and started to bawl his head off. He made so much noise that he drowned the words the shepherds were supposed to say.

Miss Clarke half rose from her seat at the piano. Sir clapped a hand to his head and told himself that it wasn't happening. Some of the audience at the back of the hall stood up to get a better view, Mrs Jefferson started moving out of her seat, and the cameraman brought his camera right up to the stage.

Then Miranda made up her mind. She came on, bringing the other two Kings with her. It was almost time for them to be on anyway and no one could hear the shepherds' last speeches through that awful racket. She went straight to the crib and lifted out her baby brother, who stopped crying at once. Holding him in her arms, she turned to Mary. 'I see your baby is giving you trouble,' she said. 'You just let me have him, ma'am. I have children of my own at home. I know what it's like.'

The audience and the rest of the cast held its

breath as Tim rose splendidly to the occasion. 'Thank you, sir,' he replied. 'You see, Mary isn't used to babies, this is her first.'

'Thank you,' said Jennifer faintly, wondering how they were ever to get back to the play as Miss Clarke had written it. 'Is that some gold you have there?'

'Gold I bring for the little King,' said Miranda, getting back into her part and using the words she had learnt. She glared at the other two Kings, who had been looking on in amazement, and this reminded them that they had words to say as they presented their gifts to Mary and Joseph. Then Annalise entered to tell them to avoid Herod's court and go home by another way and the play came to an end. As the cast lined up to bow, Miranda put the now gurgling Dominic into Jennifer's arms and stepped back to take her place with the other kings.

The audience clapped and cheered and the television crew was delighted at the sudden turn of events. 'You'll be seeing yourselves on Monday,' they promised as they left.

Dominic was restored to his mother while the cast changed and then went to join their parents for tea and cakes at the back of the hall. Charlie was jubilant. 'Couldn't have been better,' he said.

Then Lucinda appeared. 'Sir is looking for you,' she told him.

'Oh, gosh.' Charlie suddenly realized how grown-ups might look at it – bringing a live baby on to the stage without telling anybody. He wormed his way through the crowd and stood in front of Sir.

'You and Miranda ought to be punished for this,' Sir began. 'But as usual I am outvoted and you have a band of loyal supporters, including the baby's father.'

'His father!' gasped Charlie.

A tall man stepped forward, 'Yes,' he said. 'I'm Dominic's father. I was in the bedroom when

Miranda came in, and she told me what she was going to do. It seemed like a good idea to me, so I said go ahead.'

'I'm sorry he yelled so much,' said Mrs Jefferson. 'But he wasn't bad for his first acting part.'

Sir cast his eyes towards the ceiling. 'What can I do,' he asked, 'when the whole family is on their side?'

'There's nothing you can do,' said Mrs Robinson, who was standing beside him. 'Charlie will always be Charlie, and now he's been joined by Miranda, anything could happen.'

'Well, thank goodness the holidays begin on Tuesday,' said Mr McKay. 'Whatever happens in the next three weeks, it won't be my responsibility.'

The Battle of the Buns

'Can we do some acting?' asked Charlie one day in the Easter term.

'Please, Miss Clarke,' said Miranda.

Ever since their successful Nativity Play at Christmas, the Lower Juniors had decided that acting was their favourite lesson.

'All right,' said Miss Clarke. 'How would you like to do a bit of acting and learn some history at the same time?'

'History's boring,' said Charlie.

'Who says so?' asked Miss Clarke. 'Come on, get your coats, we'll go to the Coomb and have a look at the castle.'

'It's only a ruin,' said Robert when the class had arrived at the tumbledown walls of Easting Castle, which stood on a hill overlooking the valley which was known locally as the Coomb.

'It is now,' agreed Miss Clarke. 'But people

used to live there, and they fought to defend it against their enemies. There was a famous battle here in 1138. I'll tell you the story and we could come up here next week and act it.'

Later that day, Charlie explained it to his family. 'I've got to have a sword,' he said, 'and a tunic. I'm one of Matilda's men and when Stephen comes up the Coomb to storm the castle, we have to help her defend it.'

'Who's Matilda?' asked Lucinda.

'Miranda,' said Charlie. 'Well, she is in the play. The real Matilda was Henry I's daughter. When he died, the barons didn't want her to be queen.'

'Why not?' asked Lucinda.

'They didn't like her husband, and anyway, they thought a woman wouldn't be any good in charge of the country. They wanted Stephen instead. He was her cousin.'

'Cheek,' said Lucinda.

'Well, they had a war, and people took sides and everyone in Easting was on Matilda's side.'

'Who won in the end?'

Charlie pulled a face. 'Stephen,' he said. 'He captured Easting Castle and after some more battles they made him king.'

Lucinda laughed. 'You're on the losing side, Charlie Robinson.'

It was Lucinda's laugh that did it. Charlie decided that he wasn't going to be on the losing side. Somehow, he and Tim and Miranda and the others had got to stop Christopher Dodds and his lot from capturing Easting Castle, in spite of what the history books said.

Tim was enthusiastic and so was Miranda. They called their group together at playtime and Charlie explained what they were going to do. 'Whatever happens,' he said, 'we mustn't be tricked into going out of the castle and we'll have to look out for people attacking us in the rear.'

'Shall we have weapons?' asked Annalise.

'Let's have a hand-to-hand battle,' said Tim. 'We've got most of the tallest ones in our group, except Annalise.'

'If anyone fights me, I'll bite them,' said Annalise.

'She's got very sharp teeth,' said Tim.

'We could have a pile of stones,' suggested Johnnie Norbut.

'No stones,' said Miranda firmly. 'Lumps of mud if you like.'

The whistle went for the end of play and there was no time to decide any more.

'Think about it,' said Charlie, 'and if anyone lets on to the other side, I'll bash their head in.'

No one had any very useful ideas when they met the next day and they spent most of playtime listening to some news which Robert had brought to school. His father had been driving his Post Office van on the morning delivery down Western Lane when he had to stop short. One of Mr Ford's tractors was halted across the road, and Jenkins's bakery van was on its side in the ditch. 'There were loaves of bread and buns all over the place,' said Robert. 'Dad loaded them into his van and took the driver to hospital to have his arm Xrayed, and left the buns at the baker's.'

'What happened to the van?' asked Annalise.

'Luther moved it with his crane and the breakdown van,' said Robert.

That weekend, he took Charlie and Tim and Annalise up the lane to see the damage. 'You can still see the skid marks,' he said, 'and the hedge is all torn up.'

'Hey! Come over here,' called Tim, who had gone off to explore on his own in the field on the other side of the hedge. He was standing on the rim of a grassy hollow, looking down at a couple of trays which had shed their load of buns and doughnuts all over the grass at the bottom.

'Food!' shrieked Annalise and scrambled down among the doughnuts. She bit into one and pulled a face. 'They're stale,' she said. 'Still, I can lick the jam.'

Tim tried a bun. 'Rock hard,' he said in disgust. 'What a waste! Why didn't we come the day of the accident?' He threw the bun away and it hit Charlie on the arm.

'Hey!' said Charlie. 'That hurt.' He picked up a doughnut and threw it at Tim. It hit him on the side of the head and jam ran down his face.

'It looks like blood,' said Annalise.

'I've got it!' yelled Charlie, throwing buns in all directions. 'We take all this lot home and get them rock hard and we'll use them in our play to keep Christopher Dodds's gang out of the castle.'

'Yippee!' shouted Tim. 'Come on, let's get our go-cart, Lise, and take them down to Charlie's. His house is nearest to the castle. We'll smuggle them into the Coomb the night before the battle.'

When they told the rest of the group about their plan, Jennifer Muller had a bright idea.

'We've got about seven old tennis racquets at home,' she said. 'If I bring them, people like me who can't throw straight can hit them down on to Stephen's group with the racquets.'

'Brains,' said Tim. 'And we'll hide them in the Coomb with the buns.'

'We'd better hang the buns in plastic bags inside that hollow tree by the castle,' suggested Robert. 'So the foxes don't eat them before we can use them.'

On the day of the battle, they dressed up and went with Miss Clarke to the Coomb. She left Miranda and her forces at the castle and led Christopher Dodds's group down through the Coomb to their starting position about a quarter of a mile away. Christopher was Stephen, and it was his job to creep up and lure Matilda and her men out of the castle so that they could capture it. Miss Clarke had worked it all out with the class so that nothing could go wrong. They only had to play the parts that had been given to them and history would repeat itself.

While Miss Clarke was away, the others brought the ammunition into the castle. They were only just in time. Sir had left his class with Mrs Bray in charge so that he could stroll along to the Coomb to see what Miss Clarke and the Lower Juniors were up to. As he took his position behind the castle, he wondered what Tim and Charlie were doing with all those plastic bags and tennis racquets, but before he could say anything, some of Christopher Dodds's group appeared below the castle and the drama had begun.

Susan Carter was waving a white flag. 'A parley! A parley!' she called. 'We are changing sides. Come down and we will tell you all. God save Matilda!'

Charlie counted Susan's group. 'There's five of them,' he said. 'Better watch out. Where are the others?'

'Christopher isn't there,' said Miranda. 'I bet he's going to creep up and take us in the rear.'

Charlie reorganized the forces inside the castle so that everybody was drawn up in a circle facing outwards. That way, wherever the enemy attacked, someone ought to see them.

While Miranda was having her parley with Susan Carter and refusing to send anyone down, Annalise saw something move.

'There's Christopher,' she whispered. 'He's hiding in the hollow tree.'

'There are two more of them in those bushes,' added Robert.

'They're creeping up all round us,' said Jennifer. 'They'll rush us any minute.'

'Hold your fire,' ordered Tim quietly.

Then Christopher struck. Seven of his group charged towards the castle, brandishing sticks. 'Stephen for ever!' they yelled.

'Fire!' shouted Charlie and everyone inside the castle let off a fusillade of buns.

Christopher and his group checked in alarm as buns hailed down on them. Then they threw down their weapons and picked up fallen buns and began to lob them back, but they had no tennis racquets and Miranda's group were able to hit harder. Rained on by buns from all sides, Stephen's army retreated into the bushes to discuss what to do next. Charlie unfurled a Union Jack and leaped on to the wall. 'Matilda for ever!' he cried. 'Long live Queen Matilda.'

'They didn't have Union Jacks in those days,' said Tim.

'It's the only one I could find,' panted Charlie. 'Quick, everyone. Grab those buns before the others can get them.'

It was good advice, because Christopher's men burst out of the bushes to make one more attack, and they were met with such a barrage of buns that they ran away and left Miranda victorious and still in control of her castle.

Miss Clarke decided it was time to intervene. 'As this has to be a bloodless battle,' she said, 'I have to say that Matilda won on points. But it was all wrong. Why ever didn't you give in? Whose idea was all this?'

Everybody looked at Charlie. 'I didn't want to be on the losing side,' he said.

Sir's eyes twinkled. 'I might have known it was Charlie who was re-writing history,' he said. Then his expression changed and he put on his fierce look. 'However, the purpose of acting out history is to help you remember exactly what happened. Now I suppose you will all grow up thinking that Matilda won the battle of Easting Coomb.'

'No, we won't, sir,' Tim assured him, 'because Charlie organized this bit of history and we all know he isn't any good at it.'

Charlie and the Bed Race

Charlie came back from school in a very bad mood. 'It's not fair,' he said, and he slapped peanut butter two centimetres thick on his bread.

'What isn't?' asked his mother, as she handed out cups of tea.

'It's the Bed Race,' explained Lucinda. 'Sir said the Top Juniors could go in for it. There are five beds, so we can all enter if we go in groups. I'm going with Sally and Susan Patterson.'

'Yes, and he won't let the Lower Juniors have a go,' complained Charlie. 'It's not fair.'

'He says you're too young and would have accidents or not be able to finish the race,' said Lucinda.

'He might be right,' agreed Mrs Robinson. 'You can always go and watch, Charlie.'

Charlie's eyes smouldered. 'I don't want to watch,' he said. 'I want to be in it.'

The Burracombe Bed Race was held every year on the second Saturday in June. People who entered it had to push a bed on wheels over a five mile course which ran all round the reservoir, and there was a children's race of two miles. Everyone who entered was sponsored and the money went to charity.

Charlie complained to his father when he came home from work. Mr Robinson was in a very good mood because all three of his Driving School pupils who had taken their tests that afternoon had passed. He looked at Charlie's scowling face.

'Shut up a minute, Charlie,' he said, 'and listen. Anyone can enter that race, can't they, so long as they have a bed on wheels?'

'Yes,' said Charlie.

'Well,' said his father, 'why don't you enter privately with a gang of your horrible friends?'

'They're not horrible,' said Charlie. 'That's brilliant, Dad. Could we really?'

'So long as their parents don't mind, you can go ahead. Get an entry form from the shop and enter yourselves for the Children's Race.'

'What about a bed, Dad? Could I take mine?'

'Of course not, it's too clumping heavy. Use the camp bed under the stairs.'

'What about wheels?' asked Charlie.

'That's up to you. Get yourself some wheels and a gang of pushers, and I'll donate the bed and ten pence a mile for each of you.'

'Oh boy!' Charlie galumphed round the room. 'We'll get the wheels from Luther. I'll go and find the others. Mum!' he yelled as he rushed through the house. 'Will you sponsor me? I'm going to be in the Bed Race.'

A door slammed and Charlie had gone. Mrs Robinson came into the sitting room. She raised her eyebrows. 'Do you think he'll be all right?' she asked.

'Of course he will,' said Mr Robinson. 'Let him have a bit of fun. We'll be around to keep an eye on them on the day.'

Five of them walked up the lane to Luther's junk yard.

'How are we going to get the bed on to the wheels?' asked Robert.

'That'll depend on the wheels,' said Tim. 'You know, whether they're separate ones on a couple of axles or whether they're joined together on a sort of wheelbase.'

'Perhaps Luther'll help us,' said Miranda.

'Depends on what sort of mood he's in,' said Charlie.

'How do we get the bed to Burracombe?' asked Annalise. 'We'll be too tired to take it round the lake if we have to push it there first.'

'It goes there on a truck,' said Charlie.

'Whose truck?' asked Miranda.

'Dunno,' said Charlie. 'I hadn't thought about that.'

'Let's ask Jonah,' suggested Robert. 'When we've got the wheels.'

'Everyone's asking for wheels,' grumbled Luther when they found him. 'How big's this bed of yours?'

'Seventy centimetres by a hundred and eighty,' said Miranda who had had the sense to call in and measure it before going to the junk yard.

'At least it's smaller than some,' said Luther.

'It's a camp bed,' said Charlie.

'I've got some pram wheels,' said Luther. 'Come and look at them.'

They followed him past a rusting milk float, a London taxi painted bright pink, a couple of broken tractors and a jumble of refrigerators and spin dryers. At last they came to what he was looking for. Piled nearly as high as Tim himself, who was a head and shoulders taller than anyone else, was a stack of pram wheels. Some were separate, others were in pairs, and a few had enough bits of pram stuck to them to hold all four wheels together.

'What do you think?' asked Luther.

'They're all too narrow,' said Tim.

Luther took a steel tape out of his trousers pocket and laid it along one of the axles. 'You're right,' he said. 'Come on.'

He turned right at the London taxi, left round a couple of dumper trucks, and led them to a trailer which had a wooden floor and two wheels with mudguards.

'That's it,' said Charlie.

Luther took out his steel measure again. 'Hold that end for me, Charlie, will you?' he said. He bent down and grunted over the tape. 'It's big enough,' he announced.

'Super,' said Tim.

'I shall want it back,' said Luther, looking fierce, 'in the same condition it's in now.' He paused. 'I ought to ask for a deposit.'

There was a terrible silence while everyone calculated how much pocket-money they had.

'I'll leave my watch with you in exchange for the wheels,' offered Tim. 'It's a good one,' he added, 'so I shall want it back in the same condition it's in now.'

They all held their breath as they wondered whether Tim had gone too far. Then Luther grinned.

'All right, young Tim Crossman. You can take these wheels and you're in charge of them. I don't want your watch. I know where you live, and when that Bed Race is over, I'll be round to your dad if you don't bring these wheels back pronto.'

'Thanks, Luther,' said Tim.

Luther tied a rope to both ends of the trailer so that two people could pull it and the others could hang on at the back to act as a brake when they went down hill.

'Now let's go and see Jonah,' said Charlie. But Tim, looking at the watch he hadn't had to pawn, discovered that it was later than they'd realized, so they took the truck into Tim's garden and separated for the night.

Lucinda told Sir in class that Charlie and his friends were going to run in the Bed Race.

'Have they all got their parents' permission?' asked Mr McKay.

'Yes,' said Lucinda.

'That's all right then,' he said. 'They can run in as many Bed Races as they like and good luck to them, so long as they're not my responsibility.'

'They'll make a mess of it,' said Lucinda. 'And they'll come in last, I expect. They won't beat any of the Top Juniors anyway.'

But when Jonah saw Luther's wheels, he was quite sure they would win.

'That's a good base you've got there,' he said, 'pneumatic tyres and all. She'll run like a dream.'

'I wish we didn't have to pull it,' said Robert. 'If the others don't hang on to their end properly, it runs into our heels.'

After examining the trailer more closely. Jonah decided that he could fit a metal rod and bar as a handle so that it could be pushed along the road. He also said that the best way to fix the bed was to use metal clamps.

'But Luther'll be mad if we start making holes,' said Charlie.

'I'll manage Luther,' grinned Jonah. 'I'm seeing him tomorrow about borrowing his crane. Leave it to me.'

They left it to him, and when they went back, they found the handle in place and the bed clamped to the floor.

'Firm as a rock,' said Jonah. 'Who's riding in the bed?'

'Me!' shouted Annalise.

'Lazy,' said Tim. 'Still, you are the smallest and the lightest.'

'What are we going as?' said Robert. 'There's a prize for the best fancy dress.'

'Annalise can be the patient, and I'll dress up as the nurse,' said Miranda.

'We've got some tubing at home,' said Robert. 'We can make stethoscopes and be doctors.'

'Everyone'll go as doctors and nurses,' said Charlie. 'I wish we could think of something else.'

'Couldn't I be an Eastern lady like the telly advert and sit and eat Turkish Delight and you could all be my slaves?' said Miranda.

'We couldn't get the costumes,' said Charlie, who didn't fancy being anybody's slave. So they dressed up as a medical team, and Annalise used up all the crimson lake in her paintbox to make bloodstained bandages to wear on any part of herself which appeared above the bedclothes. Miranda pointed out that people didn't wear bloodstained bandages in modern hospitals.

'It's the casualty department,' said Annalise.

Charlie and the Bed Race

'People are awfully bloody in casualty departments.'

Jonah took their bed to Burracombe with his tractor. They all wanted to ride on the trailer, but he said it wasn't allowed, so they had to go in their parents' cars. It seemed that practically every tractor, truck and lorry in the area had been commandeered to transport beds to the lake. Police were directing the traffic and once the beds were in place, all the vehicles had to be left in a huge field which acted as a temporary car park.

All the children were lined up at their starting place under the watchful eye of Tony Lampeter, the Youth Club Leader from Westing. Tony explained that their route was marked out for them by yellow flags. The adults' route was marked by red ones.

'Don't run so fast that your bed gets out of control,' he warned. 'There are plenty of stewards along the way to help you if you're in trouble, and there are members of St John's Ambulance teams if anyone hurts themselves, which I hope you won't.'

Charlie could see the familiar black and white uniforms of St John, and he counted at least three ambulances in the car park.

'Only a real daftie would hurt themselves in this race,' he said. 'It's safe as houses.'

Tim grinned. 'So long as everyone can steer,' he said. 'If we collide, it might not be so good.'

They looked anxiously at some large boys from Westing who were already careering about with their beds for practice, before the race began. But fortunately they counted as adults, and the adult race was going to begin ten minutes before the children set off.

Sir came up to see how the Top Juniors were getting on. 'Good luck,' he said. Then he looked at Charlie and his friends. 'I hope you can control that thing.'

'We can, Sir,' Tim assured him.

'It's a super runner,' added Charlie.

Sir turned his back on them and spoke to Tony. 'I hope you'll keep an eye on that little group,' they heard him say. 'I didn't want any of the younger ones to take part, but I can't go against their parents. Of course, the ultimate responsibility is theirs, but still – ' He shrugged his shoulders.

'I'll be following them along the road,' Tony replied, 'and their parents are around to pick up the pieces.'

'Listen to that,' whispered Miranda crossly.

'Who do they think we are, babies?'

'We'll show 'em,' said Charlie. 'We'll beat that Top Junior lot . . . somehow,' he added, remembering that Lucinda was the fastest runner in the school.

'Let's bump them, like they do in car chases on the films,' said Robert.

'They wouldn't let us,' said Tim, 'and anyway, we'd bust up old Luther's cart.'

'Don't tip me out,' said Annalise anxiously.

'I'd like to see the ambulance men's faces if we had to take you to them,' chuckled Tim.

'Look out,' said Robert. 'The adults are off,' and they all joined in with the cheering.

Ten minutes later they were under starter's orders themselves. 'You understand what you have to do?' asked Tony. 'Just follow the yellow flags. When you finish the course, the stewards will take your names and give you your times. Remember that winning the race isn't as important as just getting to the finish,' he added, 'and the stewards will be looking out for any bad driving, so go carefully.'

There was some delay while all the beds were lined up, and then they were off.

Both Lucinda and Charlie made a good start,

but Lucinda's wheels weren't as steady as his and Charlie's team were able to keep up with her.

'We can pass her, I reckon,' gasped Charlie.

'No,' advised Tim. 'Stay behind, like Seb Coe, and then kick at the last minute and pass her down the straight.'

'Look out,' said Miranda. 'Two more coming up fast.' A bed pushed by a team from Westing passed Charlie and Lucinda at the gallop, and a second bed, steered by some of the Top Juniors, arrived and kept pace with Charlie.

'Give over, Charlie Robinson,' yelled Pete Blakeman, who was pushing.

'Not on your life,' said Charlie, 'Come on, Tim.'

But Pete Blakeman's wheels were better even than Charlie's, or maybe he had more weight to push with and longer legs, because his team spurted away from both Charlie and Lucinda.

'There's one fallen out behind us,' said Robert. 'And another. No, it's coming on, but they can't steer it properly.'

'They won't catch us,' said Tim confidently. 'It's only Lucinda now. We've got to beat her then we'll be in third place.'

'Let's go for bronze,' said Miranda. 'Come on, it's no good hanging about. Lucinda's wheels are getting wobblier by the minute. She's holding us back.'

With whoops and yells, they passed Lucinda, and the spectators gave them an encouraging cheer. Then they turned a corner and came to a short stretch of road where there were no beds in sight, and no spectators except one who was sitting on a pile of stones nursing his right ankle.

'It's Sir!' said Charlie, and they raced up to him.

'What's up, Sir?' asked Tim.

Mr McKay stood up, and as he put his right foot to the ground, he winced. 'I've twisted my ankle,' he said. 'Fell over that pile of rubble while I was looking back to see who was coming. I can't walk. Can you go on and find a steward and ask him to send a St John's Ambulance person down?'

Miranda smiled. 'Get up, Lise,' she said. 'Come on, Sir, here's a bed for you.'

Sir looked as if he'd rather not, but it did seem a sensible idea, so he hopped up to the bed and lowered himself carefully on to it.

'Do you want to borrow some of my bandages?' asked Annalise.

'No thank you,' said Sir. 'I wouldn't deprive you. You look very nice as the walking wounded.'

Then Lucinda's team came up.

'What's happened?' she asked.

'I've joined your brother's team in the Bed Race, it seems,' said Sir. 'Come on, let's get to the finishing line, my ankle's beginning to swell.'

They set off, pushing the beds side by side until one of Lucinda's wheels collapsed completely, and a steward and some spectators ran out of the crowd to help her move it to the side of the road. 'Lucinda's team can join ours,' said Charlie.

'The more the merrier,' agreed Sir.

'Are you all right, Mr McKay?' asked the steward.

'No,' replied Sir. 'But this conveyance will get me to a stretcher faster than anything else around here until we can get the cars out of the car park.'

They finished third to cheers and congratulations, and there was a lot of laughter when people realized they had their headmaster in the bed. They won first prize for costumes. 'There were a lot of hospital beds,' remarked the judge, 'but this was the only one which had a real patient.'

Sir looked at Charlie and the others. 'It seems that some of the Lower Juniors aren't so young and helpless after all,' he said.

'We're almost Top Juniors anyway, Sir,' said Charlie. 'I'm in your class next term.'

'Don't remind me,' groaned Sir.